A MOTLEY MISCELLANY

MISFIT POEMS THAT FIT TOGETHER

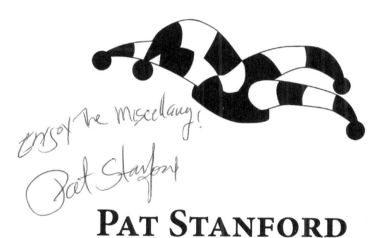

Enjoy the Miscellany!

Pat Stanford

PAT STANFORD

DocUmeant *Publishing*
244 5th Avenue
Suite G-200
NY, NY 10001
646-233-4366
www.DocUmeantPublishing.com

Published by
DocUmeant Publishing
244 5th Avenue, Suite G-200
NY, NY 10001
646-233-4366

Cover Design by: Babski Creative Studios

Layout & Illustrations by: Ginger Marks
DocUmeant Designs
www.DocUmeantDesings.com

ISBN13: 9781950075201 ($14.95 USD)

This second published volume of poetry is dedicated to my mother Evelyn Blyler Hookstra, whose poems appear for the first time in print within their own section. Since they were mostly written before she married, the section is titled with her unmarried name. Her simple little poems inspired me to begin writing at a young age and I've continued to enjoy the process throughout my life.

CONTENTS

List of Contributors in the "Pietry" Section

ZELLE ANDREWS, a FAPA award winning author, can be connected with at www.facebook.com/zelleandrews

ELIZABETH BABSKI is an award-winning graphic designer, artist, and writer. You can find her at www.babskicreativestudios.com

MARK BARIE is an award-winning author of Historical Fiction and is one of nine children. He can be reached on his website at www.Markbarie.com

MELODY BARTON BRAGG is author of three books and is a holistic psychotherapist. For more information check out her website www.thedrmelanieshow.com

DANA L. BROWN is an award-winning author of AMI Series. You can find her at info@danalbrownbooks.com

GINA EDWARDS is an author, creativity coach, and writing retreat leader. For more information, visit her website at www.AroundTheWritersTable.com

LYLA F. ELLZEY is published in a number of anthologies and has won awards for both short stories and novel-length fiction. You can contact her at: lyla.ellzey@gmail.com

RENEE GARRISON is an award-winning author who loves chocolate and coffee. Follow her on Facebook.com/anchorclankers or visit her website: www.reneegarrison.com

KEN JOHNSON is an award-winning author on culture, conflict, commerce, and conservation. He can be emailed directly at kjohnson@hhbooks.com

SAUNDRA G KELLEY, author, poet, and storyteller, can be found at her website, www.saundrakelley.com

KATHRYN KNIGHT writes as KI Knight and is an International Award-winning author, genealogist, and historian. She can be reached at www.firstfreedompublishing.com

SUSAN MAGERS is an award-winning author and special education advocate. Learn more at www.iepforparents.com

GINGER MARKS is a multi-award-winning author, designer, and publisher who writes business related books, and in 2019 she published her first children's book. She is the founder of DocUmeant Publishing & DocUmeant Designs

ROCKY PORCH MOORE is a multi-award-winning Southern Gothic author. For more information, email rockyporchmoore @gmail.com

JENNIFER "JENN" SMITH is a publishing entrepreneur and International Society of Poets fellowship winner. You can find more about her and her endeavors at MyiDealPublishing.com

KAY WHITEHOUSE is a multi-awarding-winning author who has been awarded the Gold Award of Excellence by Mom's Choice. Kay can be reached at whitehousekay12@gmail.com

JANE R. WOOD is the author of a series of books where she weaves history and science into stories for young readers, and one nonfiction book. You can learn about Jane and her books at www.janewoodbooks.com

Introduction

This collection of poems was hanging out on my hard drive with no obvious place to put them. None of the individual groupings had enough in them to each make their own volume. What to do with them? Well, I ignored them for the longest time, but *they* had heard that some of their *friends* had been published and they kept bugging me to do that for them too. So here they are, a Motley Bunch, all!

Explaining the Sections

It isn't often one is challenged to write a poem a day for a month, but I was during National Poetry Month of April of 2020, which also happened to be during the Covid-19 Coronavirus Pandemic. The first section of this collection is of those written during that time—*Poems Penned in a Pandemic* and while not all of them are *about* the virus, many of the other topics written during that time were *affected by* it. For example, I may not have been moved to write poems about Holy Week if I was able to attend church to celebrate it. By the same token, I may not have even thought about writing a few about my garden if the pandemic hadn't made me stir crazy enough to start working more days in it.

I used to write a *lot* of songs when I was a teen, but never really did anything with them because I always thought I was too young and inexperienced to send them off to be recorded. Still, their poetry remains behind. Aside from them, I included some silly stuff that I write once in a while. Where to put these? With other poems that don't "fit" anywhere else—*A Motley Miscellany*. If you buy me a scotch or two, I might sing the songs for you. Off key, probably.

A group of "orphan poems" started out with the intention of being part of a collection about various real pets and my "stuffed animals" (AKA "plush toys"). Some of the poems were robbed from their original collection to include in *Proverbs of My Seasons; Poetry of Transition*. The remnant of the original collection is titled *Menagerie of Memory*. It reminds us that while we have to give up toys, and our pets eventually die, they *do* live on in our memory.

I came to poetry quite naturally. My mother penned her poetry in cloth bound "Scribble In Books." She wrote simple little ditties, but she had fun with them as she wrote them in ink color to match the color of the cover. (yes, really) They are in the order (dated of course), in which she scribbled them. I include hers with this volume simply as *Evelyn Blyler's Poetry*. I always wanted to have them published, even though she might be mortified, yet blissfully unaware that they are now "out there." I was tempted to "correct" them so they would flow better but, if I did that, then they would no longer be Evelyn Blyler's poetry, so, I left them exactly as she wrote them in her little blank book.

The last collection *Pietry; A Literal Literary Feast* began as a private message from an author friend, congratulating me on the publishing of my first book of poetry. Only she mistyped it and it came out "pietry." After having some laughs and ribbing her with other friends on social media, a new word emerged. I asked my friends for their favorite pie recipe and to write a poem about it. I told them I would include it in this collection if they did. Really, it was just a sneaky way to get their recipes. Most of the pie-ets have probably not written poetry since grade school, but they had fun doing it.

By the way, after you hit the wrong key *one time*, while trying to type the word "poetry" it is almost automatic that it becomes "pietry" every time!

Enjoy the poems, piems and pies!

POEMS PENNED IN A PANDEMIC

COVID ADVENTURE

It was my weekly trip to Publix
to get my usual few things.
I hoped they'd have some chicken;
nope, just frozen chicken wings.

I really didn't need that much
just restocking here and there.
Although the store just opened
there were people everywhere.

"Prepping for the Zombie Apocalypse?"
I thought as I watched a cart roll by.
And just what *is* it about toilet paper?
Nobody I've asked really knows why.

Got that covered last month at Costco
but is it enough? I begin to doubt.
Everyone has some in their buggies
and I don't want to be the one left out!

Got a brisket to celebrate St. Pats Day.
So what if it is almost a week later?
No cabbage on the shelf to go with it;
sauerkraut works, added in with taters.

I'll leave with money still in the bank
still pondering TP in the checkout line.
The pull toward that aisle is very strong
others need a year's supply, but I'm fine.

Stanford, P. (2020) *Variegated Verses in a Millennial Age.*
Florida: Independently published.

A COVID Haiku Progression

Hey Covid-19?
It's not you making me cough.
It's just the pollen.

Hubby is sent home
to work in our spare bedroom.
Where will I go now?

Perhaps my roses
have missed me; they seem happy
book fairs are cancelled.

Out in my garden
I ponder toilet paper
among pretty blooms.

THEME PARK

Grocery stores are theme parks now;
everyone wants to go.
Big attractions on every aisle.
Why this is, I simply don't know.

Families show up as a whole
not just a mom or dad.
I guess they have cabin fever—
has it really gotten that bad?

STAY

Stay at home today
is an order we were told.
Only essentials—
food, gas, Fluffy to the vet,
then back to cleaning closets.

PALM SUNDAY
(A SERIOUS LIMERICK)

I wonder what this day will bring
as I listen to little birds sing.
I allow myself to smile
forgetting strife for a while
knowing Jesus is still Lord and King!

Tenebrae

Light is extinguished,
slowly casting strange shadows
on the Savior's cross
until it is clear to us
why He endured in the dark.

WISTFUL PATIENCE

I want to see your garden
and for you to come see mine.
We show pics on Facebook
and yes, that's all just fine.

But I want to touch your cactus
and for you to smell a rose
that I fertilized and watered
and you take home one of those.

I'd like to come hug your neck
or maybe just shake your hand.
It'd be like old times then;
but that's not the law of the land.

It'd be nice to meet for coffee
instead of Face Time or on Zoom.
or go to the theater to watch a movie
instead of Netflix in my bedroom.

I know we'll do all these again
and don't think it's as bad as it seems.
Keep safe and well, my friends—
meantime, I'll see you in my dreams.

Stanford, P. (2020) *Variegated Verses in a Millennial Age.*
Florida: Independently published.

———. (2020) *Pandemic in Paradise: Florida Stories from the 2020 Coronavirus Pandemic.* Florida: Independently published.

In Want of Coffee During COVID-19

While I wait service on my car,
I've got my pick of seats.
Sitting in the waiting room;
with no coffee and no treats

There is one other person here—
she's got a steaming mug;
she brought it in from home.
The look from her was smug.

I went out to look at other cars
just for something to do.
Got my steps in for the day
but can't wait til I am through.

FLAT LINE

Staying at home to flatten the curve,
watching the news every night;
hoping by diligence we will succeed
and all this will come out all right.

A week to be reckoned with
so say all the outlets hawking news.
Hoping against hope it's not so,
yet it's not a thing we can choose.

Some will be dead by months end
while most will come out just fine;
while we wait for the curve to turn,
they'll see a different flat line.

Stanford, P. (2020) *Variegated Verses in a Millennial Age.*
Florida: Independently published.

FREE

Why is it called Good Friday?
Wasn't it a really bad day
for Jesus so long ago
taking care of a debt to pay?

It never was about Him;
it was all meant for mankind;
we who deserve nothing
we, the deaf and the blind.

Why is it called Good Friday?
What's in it for you and me?
It shows the depth of God's love
to make us eternally free.

Stanford, P. (2020) *Variegated Verses in a Millennial Age.*
Florida: Independently published.

ANTICIPATION

A day to reflect
before glory is revealed.
Anticipation,
leaving us both excited
and humbled by tomorrow.

TAX DAY TANKA

Here it is Tax Day:
even that's changed for this year;
longer to file them.
Does that mean more interest?
The stimulus won't help much.

Stanford, P. (2020) *Variegated Verses in a Millennial Age*.
Florida: Independently published.

QUARANTINE

The house is immaculate.
All closets are clean;
the garden is planted
and all seems serene.

A new painting is started;
a new short story too.
A poem, a novel,
a long list of "to do".

If everything gets done,
what else will we start
while keeping a distance
of six feet apart?

We long for the old days
which may never be seen,
when we are released
from this long quarantine.

Stanford, P. (2020) *Variegated Verses in a Millennial Age.*
Florida: Independently published.

HALLELUJAH

What could I possibly write
on this day of glory revealed?
It has all been said before
about a tomb now unsealed.

What could I possibly add?
I have no original song.
I can only stand in awe;
add my voice to the throng:
Hallelujah!

STIMULUS

Sometime in the night
it snuck in my bank account.
Bills paid for the month
but none left for my own fun;
I am not stimulated.

Stanford, P. (2020) *Variegated Verses in a Millennial Age.*
Florida: Independently published.

LANDSCAPE LIMERICK

My roses began to look better.
I dunno if it's cuz they are wetter,
or if they began to succeed
due to my weeding and feed
and a spray plan done to the letter.

POSITIVE IMPACT

What occupies your time
during this pandemic, this horrid thing
we are enduring together?

Learning to cook for the first time
or hitting the local take out lines
to help restaurants stay in business?

Planting some veggies in your side yard
to get a feeling for mother earth
while learning to take care of yourself?

Playing games with your children
and reconnecting since those days
seldom existed when you left for work?

Painting something new on a canvas
and becoming someone different
and renewed, not afraid to emerge?

Goofing off for hours on social media
and arguing with people you don't know
about everything and absolutely nothing?

Resting and reflecting on what's important
so you'll know what to rush back to (or not)
when we get back to whatever normal is.

What occupies your time
does not have to define who you are;
but can, if you're brave enough to change.

Stanford, P. (2020) *Variegated Verses in a Millennial Age*. Florida: Independently published.

ABSENCE OF NORMALCY

In the absence of normalcy
we try to acquire
something not of ourselves
but that we may desire.

Not a usual thing
though buried deep within;
a talent we've held back
or were too busy to begin.

In the absence of normalcy
we can redefine who we are!
Why don't we do that anyway—
does it seem all that bizarre?

Stanford, P. (2020) *Variegated Verses in a Millennial Age.*
Florida: Independently published.

Hot Day

Springtime or Summer?
The heat and pressure are up,
and it feels like rain.

OPEN

With nine hundred deaths
are we certain it is time
to open things up?

In Want of a Secret Garden

I had a dream two nights ago
where I was toiling with a hoe
and shovel, rake and clippers too
to make a garden—one brand new;
From underbrush so overgrown
I'd make this spot all my own;
a place to come and read a book,
or to contemplate there in my nook.

Yesterday I began the ardent chore
to create a thing that never before
had been in that particular spot.
I worked 'til I became quite hot,
and wondered who would ever care.
Who might come visit me there?
But I should not think of others feet
ever finding my little secret retreat.

Stanford, P. (2020) *Variegated Verses in a Millennial Age.*
Florida: Independently published.

Cheapest Bidder

My hubby still works from home;
he's on the job at 8 on the nose;
a considerable savings on gas
and lessened washing of clothes.

I've become a bit of an assistant
but I did not ask for the position.
It's fine—it makes it easier for him
but tends to be a source of friction.

The state is known for low pay;
that's something they should consider
while my own daily schedule suffers,
I may qualify as their cheapest bidder.

POWER

Tornadoes and rain,
heavy lightning lit the sky;
power crews at work.
Something else to talk about
besides Covid-19.

HALFWAY HAIKU

Today marks halfway
of April Poetry Month.
Why don't you try one?

IN THE GARDEN
(A NEW TAKE ON AN OLD CLASSIC HYMN)

I sit on my porch in the morn
with a tumbler of coffee in hand.
Crisp air and a breeze rustling through the trees
feels like a subtle command.

When I get up to walk in my garden
my voice joins a familiar song
given to me by the One I can't see,
yet His presence is felt so strong.

Birds suddenly stop their chirping
and I wonder why that might be so?
Dew on a bloom; its scent of perfume
makes my heart so want to know.

Returning from 'Rona

The 'Rona gave us quite a scare;
it took many lives and that's not fair.
For healthy people, death is rare
but older people should take care.
If the nation would be in prayer
then there is no need to despair.
We should still continue to be aware;
jammies won't be what we can wear
when we're released from couch and chair,
to live good lives again, if we dare.

Stanford, P. (2020) *Variegated Verses in a Millennial Age.* Florida: Independently published.

———. (2020) *Pandemic in Paradise: Florida Stories from the 2020 Coronavirus Pandemic.* Florida: Independently published.

Essential

Essential activities—what are they?
Do you understand the new order yet?
Go to doctors, get gasoline and food;
Oh, and you can take Fido to the vet.

Essential places—where are they?
Liquor stores are curiously included.
Is a park or a lake high on this list,
or are they not sufficiently secluded?

Essential people—who are they?
People whose work is relied upon,
yet, to a family, "essential" means more
especially if a parent's job is now gone.

We are all essential, but don't get the label
since being restricted really isn't so tough.
I don't worry that I'm home waiting this out;
I'm not essential, but I am enough.

Stanford, P. (2020) *Variegated Verses in a Millennial Age.*
Florida: Independently published.

———. (2020) *Pandemic in Paradise: Florida Stories from
the 2020 Coronavirus Pandemic.* Florida: Independently
published.

GOODBYE TO POETRY MONTH

Someone said this was easy—
writing a poem every day;
but I am here to tell you
it's hard finding new things to say.
Something different or funny
or maybe a tad profound.
Mostly don't come natural,
some take work to expound.

So here I am celebrating
National Poetry Month's ending.
I can get back to other things;
no longer a poet pretending.
While there's still yard work to do
I may not find that exciting.
Now that this challenge is over
I can get back to novel writing!

Stanford, P. (2020) *Variegated Verses in a Millennial Age.*
Florida: Independently published.

A Motley Miscellany

Goodbye to Blue Elephants and Such
Among the Stars
Out of a Position (No More Softball for Me)
Death Wish
John At 40 In '80 (For John Lennon)
The Unknown Poet
It's a College Life
Troubadour
Cocktails and Coffee
The Ritz
A Barred Variation
Money
Week in Milwaukee
See You All Again
Jamaican Sunset
No Flies On Me
I Didn't Know Her
Depression Blues
Rapture of the Road
Desperation Duet
Guys With Earrings
Tallahassee Classy
In Memory of Poets
A Fable of Warning
Ecclesiastes 1.1
Hunkered
My Days
Camelot Subdivision Hurricane Song
Hermine's Haikus
I Miss You

Precious Medals
A Tribute (Sort of)
White Crosses
I Saw Heaven Opened
I Must
Poetry
Tea Rose
Prima Donna
Growth
A Lighter Shade of Purple
Geezer
Piece of Paper

Goodbye to Blue Elephants and Such

I woke up in the morning
  and saw upon the wall
teams of crickets and roaches
  playing games with a mothball.

The score was six to nothing—
  the crickets were ahead
but when the roaches hit a home run
  it knocked me out of bed!

I sought to feed my ravaged body
  but the bread was hard and stale.
The coffee tasted much like water
  from a keg of rusty nails.

The knife and fork got spoony;
  and my cup began to spin.
When I opened up the fridge;
  that's when my knees gave in.

A leftover stone-cold T-bone
  and fuzzy-green Cheddar cheese
stared out at me from the shelves.
  That's when I began to wheeze.

I think we can all clearly see
  I can no longer hold my liquor.
Back to straight lemonade for me
  for I've never been much sicker.

AMONG THE STARS

I love to go out walking in a dense fog,
under the moonlight, by a lonely bog,
among bright stars in an inky black sky;
reminding me of saucers and wishing I could fly.

Is that a moon shadow following me,
or is it a plane that I cannot see?
(I saw it again when night came to pass
landing nearby on soft, damp grass.)

Frightened, thoughts ran rampant through my mind;
will the inhabitants there be hostile or kind?
There are so many things I don't understand;
the grey person reached out and took my hand.

Will someone wake me from this dream?
I am so afraid, but I cannot scream.
I'm excited by the glow that has me surrounded.
They lead me inside and I am further astounded.

Strong engines lift us and soon we are high;
alone at my window, I watch planets go by.
Grey people, don't take me where I should not go–
away from my world, to where cooler winds blow.

When we land, I sense I've been here before,
and realized this was what I had searched for.
Long ago, by the bog, I was left all alone;
found by two humans, into human, I'd grown.

Once I wondered of life in a strange, distant land,
thinking, "Life is more than this small, human band."
So, happy am I now on my planet beyond the sun,
where I fly among the stars that humans gaze upon.

If those on planet Earth would not be afraid,
or think the grey people are staging a raid,
new things we could show them, friends we could be
in our little galaxy ship, midst a vast planet sea.

Out of a Position
(No More Softball for Me)

My old batty name is "Flash",
my heads are made of tin and teak;
into third bagger I will crash
and all my joints will squeak.

When into the house I coast,
I then begin to wheeze;
my lungs are burned up toast,
thus, my longest word's a sneeze.

My teeth are gone for all her vice,
my hair is made of sand;
the language was not all nice,
so, the squatter and I were banned.

Fourth inning, that little sphere
came down the pipe, I hit a breeze;
the next rock, I thought was outta here,
but the grasser caught it with such ease.

A fan of fury flew from my beak,
the coacher said there was no need
to use such lingo when I speak.
I was cut, but I didn't bleed.

DEATH WISH

You can't ignore them—they won't disappear—
these reminders who have been left to die.
They still look at the world in all its madness
once a part of it, now left in hallways to cry.

People now hurry past them not seeing
huddled masses in the corners of their rooms;
unbelieving that they were once in the fray
they have little light to penetrate the gloom.

Continue to ignore them, you'll never learn
what they learned while in their prime;
this becomes a death wish if you let it
continue during your own time.

JOHN AT 40 IN '80
(FOR JOHN LENNON)

Out of a five-year seclusion, you finally came,
not to seek added fortune and fame,
but, to sing praise of happiness you had found
with a family—now complete, 'n solid ground.

To let us know that another birthday wasn't so bad
and that life lived to the fullest is never a fad;
that you removed your mask, worn for so many years;
one you had to wear to make it through your tears.

It all ended as abruptly as it had begun,
for you barely started on new songs to be sung.
Silenced now forever by an action so inane,
by one who loved you, then said he was insane.

Part of me went with you, part of me stayed,
as you did with many as they silently prayed
that you are now at peace, that is all you asked;
and we never will forget the special shadow you cast.

THE UNKNOWN POET

Snappy, snappy snapperbell . . .
I wish you'd leave me in my cell
to give me enough alone time
to write my silly little rhyme!

Grouchy, grouchy, glunkerhow . . .
I hear a constant rhythm now,
but someone soon will call my name
and make me angry once again.

Could you please leave me alone a while,
so I can write a few lines and emerge with a smile?
If you can't 'ya know, leave me alone for a few,
you could all be added to a nice beef stew.

Madly, madly, marinade . . .
I see sunrise and watch it fade;
steadily stirring my bubbling brew
of Uncle Ned and Mary Lou.

Crazy, crazy, crankyshoes . . .
in the basement, I tie a noose.
All my other actions, you won't condone,
so, as a poet, I died unknown.

It's a College Life

Got pills to alleviate the pain,
got lovers to alleviate the strain—
chain smokers, hazy tokers
all turn into Brand X chokers.

Seen midnight term paper writers,
seen daytime chronic nail biters—
weekend drunkards, all day junkards
soon turn into college flunkards.

If I hear one more lecture today,
I swear, I will take a fly
out the fourth-floor window—
I'll kiss this all goodbye!

No time to enjoy a still minute,
no friend to enjoy it with it—
back stabbers, money grabbers
keep swords in hidden scabbards.

Must always be on the wary,
hide the pride that you can't carry—
betray your friend, watch it end
up into what you will intend.

TROUBADOUR

I wish I had a troubadour
to sing a song to me;
a song that tells a story
of lonely mariners at sea.

Or about those shining knights
who were so adventuresome,
and scrapping, brawling peasants
amid a tavern full of rum.

Then on to kingly feasts,
where all there ate too much;
after parlor maids and opium
were said to be a crutch.

And I wish that troubadour
would really tell us how it was,
so we can forget our crazy times;
the drugs, free sex, the Fuzz.

Sing of better days gone by,
oh, you happy troubadour—
but, sing the truth and all will see
it is now, no worse than before.

COCKTAILS AND COFFEE

Solitaire and paperbacks,
cigarettes and beer,
whatever am I doing,
sitting alone in here?

I come to this singles bar
almost every night,
trying to find someone
I can hold tight at night.

Coffee in the morning, cocktails at night—
one gets me through the darkness, the other through
    the light.
I have nobody that I call Mr. Right,
so it's coffee in the morning, cocktails at night.

I go to work each morning
to have a little money
to get me through the week;
but, none to spend with you, honey.

I'll never know your kind,
or hold you close to me.
I wonder what it's like
to go through life so carefree.

Coffee in the morning, cocktails at night—
one gets me through the darkness, the other through
    the light.
I have nobody that I call Mr. Right,
so it's cocktails and coffee, every day and every night.

THE RITZ

The Ritz is a place you don't go every day,
it's on the shady side of town;
beer, wine, and liquor, just name your taste—
the one in which you'd like to drown.

The bartender serves 'til you can no longer see,
slipping "mickies" to girls he like the best;
talks to them til they're numb, then takes them home
and puts them in a bed, but not to rest.

All this is a cover, I really do believe
something funny's going on at the Ritz.

The same bleary-eyed people run the joint every day,
they have grass on their clothes; and that isn't hay.
For an ugly lookin' joint, it seems to do quite well;
what most folks don't know is booze ain't all they sell.

The hostess asks if you put sugar in your tea,
which sounds a bit too innocent, especially to me,
for I have been assigned to be a regular there
to blow off the lid and catch the owner in a snare.

The guy knows who I am and looks like he'll cut me
into bits;
I'm getting outta this detective job and the hell
outta the Ritz.

A Barred Variation

Starkle, starkle little twink,
you're my companion as I drink.
I'm not drunk, as peep thinkle;
I need to go, but just to tinkle.

I had only tee martoonies
but it's enough to make me looney.
Come soddenday, I'll be sorry,
but, not half as much as I'll be tomorry.

I fool feelish—I don't know who's me;
my stomach is hiding rye upon the sea.
I haven't stallen off my fool yet,
but the drunker I sit here, the longer I get.

Money

Money here, money there;
I see money everywhere.
It flows free here like the air;
still some folk don't get their share.

Money is power, money is pain;
it can bind you, like a chain
and make you become very greedy—
more for you, and less for the needy.

Some money is coarse, some quite rude,
the more I see of them—downright crude.
Having money won't make you better than me—
I don't have lots of money, but at least I am free.

WEEK IN MILWAUKEE

I had a tough week in Milwaukee,
I felt so bad, I started to cry;
so I stopped into Gold Rosey's Lounge,
'cos I was feeling mighty dry.

Sat down, ordered a Gin and Tonic;
it's always been a good old friend.
Started talkin' to the guy next to me
wonderin' where this all might end.

Well, it seems so hard to say,
but I've seen a better day.
I'm wonderin' what I am here for;
I've had enough but wanted more.

I felt no pain after a refill—
yeah, I even started to laugh.
Two guys ordered four more beers,
a lady's working on her third carafe.

Three's enough, but fours too many,
but I was feeling pretty good.
The guy then looked me in the eye
and it was clear where he thought he stood.

Well, it seems so hard to say,
but I've seen a better day;
I wondered what I was there for,
I had to leave, still wanting more.

SEE YOU ALL AGAIN

When I came back to this little town
after being gone so long,
I met some old friends at a bar
and we sang a well-known song.

I've been gone for such a long, long time
and I've been so far away.
You don't know how long I tried,
but I could no longer stay.

Gosh, it's good to see a friendly face again,
where you been, what you been up to, friend?
Remembered times we thought would never end,
and yeah, it's good to see you all again.

I wish I could have taken you with me
taken you with me on the road.
There're so many strange new people
that your old ways will soon erode.

I had just got here when I went down
went down to the town.
Talked and sang with those old pals
before I had to turn back around.

But, gosh, it's good to see a friendly face again,
where you been, what you been up to, friend?
Remembered times we thought would never end,
and yeah, it's good to see you all again.

JAMAICAN SUNSET

We met on a tropical island
where life's pressures are no longer found.
We relaxed with a Pina Colada
on a beach with nobody around.

We talked through the day into nighttime
about things that meant nothing at all.
We walked, we wondered, we daydreamed
then we spotted the blue waterfall.

To this day, I'll always remember
and I know I will never regret
the evening we spent in Kingston
beneath the Jamaican Sunset.

We stopped just to notice the beauty
of something so free and so grand
on an island so lovely, so timely
we decided that this was our land.

We pondered our future together
at the place where two lovers have met;
where the days and the nights are for dreamers
beneath the Jamaican Sunset.

To this day, I'll always remember
and I know I will never regret
the evening we spent in Kingston
beneath the Jamaican Sunset.

Co-written with Vance Fothergill providing the music.

*He sang it every night at the Cabana Club Restaurant,
Boca Raton Hotel & Resort*

No Flies On Me

You say I don't love you baby,
you say I don't really care—
but, lover boy, I really do
though I'm not always there.

But you start putting ties on me
tell me what to do and say,
I'll show you there ain't no flies on me
and Babe, I'll run away.

Ain't no flies on me baby, ain't no flies on me
Well, I move up and I move down.
I wanna tell ya baby, I get around.

Ain't about to wait around for you,
I can't take the chance.
I ain't about to stay around for you,
I'll find a new romance.

You ain't got nothin' babe
I can't find somewhere else.
I'm gonna find another man
who likes me, for myself.

You know. I see. No flies. On me.

'Aint no flies on me baby, ain't no flies on me
Well, I move up and I move down.
I wanna tell ya baby, I get around.

I Didn't Know Her

Years ago, back in high school, she came from
  another town;
I felt I'd known her forever and felt better with
  her around.
Carefree friends were all we were; never cared to be each
  other's lover.
Each shared a dream to be married but, we never
  married each other.

"You don't know me," she said, "but it's okay, we'll
  both be fine."
I never gave it too much thought but, I liked beer, she
  liked fine wine.
"I have things I've got to do before settling
  with a family;
I feel I really need to roam, while I do this, you
  won't know me."

I married, she went to college; we had a baby, she
  got a degree.
I got divorced, she got Air Forced—sad letters went
  pouring out of me.
But when she got out and came back home, I hoped
  we'd be more than friends.
I want to say I always loved her, but, to that, she
  put and end.

"You don't know me," she said. I could not marry
    you, you see.
Though I've always loved you; after ten years you still
    don't know me.
"I have things I've got to do and my love, you
    cannot see
that if I don't I won't be whole that's why, I don't
    even know me.

She's doin' things she had to do, goin' places where
    there's lots to see
but, soon I think she'll be ready, and then I'll ask her
    to marry me.
"You don't know me she said, "but, it's okay, we'll
    both be fine."
I love being best of friends—I drink my beer, she
    drinks her wine.

DEPRESSION BLUES

I got the low-down depression blues;
I'd start to cry, but what's the use?
I got no money to pay the rent
and next week's money's already spent.

I got the low-down depression blues
I'd sing sad songs, but I can't refuse
a good old-time boogie melody
that we can sing together, you and me.

It takes every damn dollar
just to get by today
Makes you scream and holler
Oh, but what can you say?

You can go downtown
you can play around
You don't need a lot of money
to act like a fool, honey.

Love the things in life that are free
and depressed you won't always be,
Depression is a state of mind.
Just laugh and life will be kind.

It takes every damn dollar
just to get by today
Makes you scream and holler
Oh, but what can you say?

RAPTURE OF THE ROAD

It's peaceful out there, just you and the trees,
the clouds, the grass, the birds and the bees.
Keep up your pace, breathe deep, fill your soul
with sweet, morning air and renewed self-control.

No need for races to speed blood through your veins—
you even feel more peaceful and purer when it rains.
When you can press yourself to your maximum load,
you will know that feeling I call rapture of the road.

DESPERATION DUET

I wrote this real neat letter
to some Nashville record studio.
My dream of being a songwriter
got to me, don't you know?

I told 'em about this real neat song
written by some reformed drunk
who met a girl on a southbound train
carrying just one travel trunk.

Well, surprise, surprise, they did reply
and said, "Send that song on up here—
sounds like a song our new star could sing."
I tell ya, I never felt more fear.

I didn't have a damn thing written;
my dream soon became a big regret.
But I sat down to blank white paper
to write my "Desperation Duet."

A friend of mine stopped by that night
and he brought a bunch of beer.
I told him about my problem—
He said, "Well, the answer's pretty clear."

"We gotta write a song for two
about them being on a train,
together on a ride to nowhere,
because their lives were down the drain."

"We have them sad and alone at first,
and then, by chance, they'll meet—
by the end of their long journey,
they'll sing happy and so sweet."

It's not such a terrible song,
but it's not a big hit yet.
But, thanks to a friend and a bunch of beer
I wrote that "Desperation Duet."

Guys With Earrings

I went out to a bar one night
just to have fun, by chance.
But then some guy came up to me
and asked if I would dance.

He had a nice enough face, all right
but the thing that turned me stale
was that he had this little gold earring
and down his back, a ponytail.

I said, "I don't dance with guys with earrings,
my men will always look like men."
Then he left with a strange expression
I'd not seen since I don't know when.

Well, he went onto the dance floor
and he wailed something out of sight.
I began thinking he's the only one
who could dance like that all night.

My feet were dancing under the table;
I wondered if I should take the chance
with this guy and his little gold earring—
If I didn't I might never dance!

I didn't dance with guys with earrings;
I thought they were a different kind,
but I watched him with the other gals,
then, I had to change my mind.

He came back near my table later,
yet he didn't ask again.
He went to the bar and ordered
a straight shot of bourbon then.

I gave up after my fifth drink
I had to know how I would do
with that maniac dancer on whisky,
I began wailing like a maniac too.

I guess I dance with guys with earrings,
they, too, can look like real men.
They don't have to be a different kind;
I had a lot of fun that night, way back when.

TALLAHASSEE CLASSY

When visiting Tallahassee
You'll want to do something classy
So, go to Chez Pierre
and partake of their fare
but it will make you quite gassy.

Note: The property that was Chez Pierre has changed hands at least twice since I wrote this and I recently had my 35th anniversary dinner there, as Table 23.

In Memory of Poets

There once were Poets of Big Bend
Who met to read poems they penned,
but too much inaction
made them a mere fraction
and caused them to come to an end.

A Fable of Warning

A long time ago, a large mountain shook and rumbled.
It heaved and sighed so intently, the people of the village
    at its feet
wondered what sort of incredible thing it would
    bring forth.
They were awed more and more each day,
as it grew bigger and bigger.
One day, it began to tremble and quake
and finally spewed forth its offspring . . .
A mouse.

The people were dumbfounded as they expected
    greatness from such effort.
They were angered at themselves for having such
    expectations.
Several years passed when a smaller mountain nearby
    heaved and sighed,
but the people paid it no mind,
for they knew only a mouse would come of it.
It rumbled and shook, and began to spew lava and fire,
which ran down the hill
while the villagers, still looking for the mouse,
were swallowed it the wake.

ECCLESIASTES 1.1

Meaningless—all is meaningless
and nothing is new under the sun.
What is now is what was before—
everything has already been done.

Vanity—all is vanity;
what do we gain from our toil?
Generations come and then they go
but remain forever on earthly soil.

Wearisome—all is wearisome;
so much more than I can say.
Eyes can't see and ears can't hear,
not nearly enough for today.

Crooked—all is crooked
and never shall be any less.
If found lacking, can't be counted;
it is all just one big mess.

Knowledge—all my knowledge
can't leave me feeling less chagrined.
Wisdom is only madness and folly,
and I still chase after the wind.

HUNKERED

We're in a storm that's true
but one thing I wish they'd do
is stop using a certain word
overused to be so absurd.

Weather-folk use it all the time;
I cringe at the continued crime
of them using the word "hunker"
while we're sheltered in our bunker.

"Make sure you hunker down,
and please don't go to town
unless an emergency so dire
makes you go out in this quagmire."

Is hunkering *up* a choice?
If so, I think I might rejoice
simply for a different expression
mid the next tropical depression.

My Days

Yep.
I am at home now and don't have to work;
I check email and do the damn dishes.
I sometimes go out.
I sometimes write.
I do laundry and groceries;
I wait for you to come home.
We go out to the porch to supposedly talk.
You text this one or that one but I'm not supposed to be
    jealous or text anyone myself.
We have dinner.
You go to sleep in your chair.
I go to bed.
Yep.

Camelot Subdivision Hurricane Song

The rain began just after noon on Thursday;
wind picked up and things quickly turned to pot.
Power went out just before the clock struck midnight
In Camelot.

Then began our wait for any 'lectric power;
We're last on the list, I really kid you not,
cuz everyone keeps posting they've got AC.
Not in Camelot!

Camelot, Camelot
I know that sounds a bit bizarre.
But in Camelot, Camelot
That's how conditions are.

More rain came Friday late before the evening;
it brought a breeze to us who are so very hot.
That sound you hear are neighbor's generators
In Camelot.

No caffeine Friday, but we fixed that problem.
A separate cord is strictly for the coffee pot.
In short, there's simply not
A more sweaty, noisy spot
while trying to get a little sleep
than here . . . in . . . Cam . . . e . . . lot!

Sung to the tune of Camelot (Penned during Hurricane Hermine)

HERMINE'S HAIKUS

My post on social media:

Lights are flickering,
and now, so are some candles.
Ready for Hermine.

Friend's responses:

Hurricane Hermine
You're a pain in the hiney!
Now we can't sit down.

Wind is really loud
I have my safe room ready
Go away Hermine!

I hear the rain now,
the wind is picking up too,
a glass of wine, please.

Transformer blowing.
Sitting in the dark not bad
Think I will eat cake

Too dark and silent
I wish I had some ice cream
Is Publix open?

I Miss You

I keep waiting for you
   to return home from work
     but you don't.

I look over to tell you
   about a funny little thing,
     but you're not there.

I turn over to touch you
   while in bed asleep,
     but, I'm alone.

I don't even get a chance
   to be ignored by you,
     if you block me out.

I have no chance to argue
   over something that used to
     start horrendous fights.

I still get a tight feeling
in my chest and get flushed
when I think of us together
  I miss you.

PRECIOUS MEDALS

What color is my medal;
is it silver, bronze or gold?
I must wait, worry, and wonder
before that will be told.

What color is the ribbon;
will it clash with my clothes,
and make me wonder why
this was the outfit I chose?

What if it is *only* bronze;
will that show me to be befitting
a special place among writers
with whom I may be sitting?

Silver is pretty, but is it the best
or should gold be what I desire?
The red ribbon it comes with
will surely go with any attire.

But that I am considered worthy
to have my name brought up at all
makes them all precious medals
and I feel like I'm ten feet tall!

Written while waiting to find out which medal I won for Poetry in 2019

A Tribute (Sort of)

The Elegy
Unbelieving the message left about your early death;
hardly imagining that you'd taken your last breath.
My soul lost a mate and there is nothing more I can do
to tell you what you meant to me before we
    were through.

You gave to me a deeper sense of what I could
    one day be
and because of you, I now am whole, or maybe
    just set free.
Crying are those who cared for you while others
    merely stare
in unbelief that your smiles are through yet seeming
    not to care.

Quietly, they lower you into the rich brown earth;
such care to have your body in the same town as
    your birth.
Your raging soul made sure to see that this final
    place of rest
be here with foe and friend, but perhaps they weren't
    your best.

That was the plan, I'm sure of it—to make each of
    them recall
your steadfast beliefs that would not change
    over *any* haul.
With you now gone, I wonder how our numbers
    shall increase;
I don't know what I'll do without you, but I know you
    are at peace.

The Dirge

We built you a monument
to weather snow, rain and tears.
A granite soldier, it will stand alone
for more than a hundred years.

But you were not that silent
and you never were alone;
always so proud and defiant.
Not resembling this solid stone.

Your rage is quiet, all is still.
You'll be heard, but not aloud.
We leave you now to peer from the weeds
around our stone tribute, silent and proud.

The Epitaph

I went to sleep
You woke me
I turned my back on you
You put a mirror before me
I started to scream
You turned it into a song.

WHITE CROSSES

Traveling across the countryside
on a bus or a car, just taking a ride;
you see them dotting any major route—
wonder if they bore any spiritual fruit.

There's "Joe" on state Road 84
and he's with the Lord forevermore.
"Steve & Cindy—Together Forever"
are marked within the roadside heather.

White Crosses mark the spot
where they made their final earthly stop.
It was, for each, a fateful day
when their lives were swept away.

Ed's cross has a hat nailed to its peak
he called in sick to go fish midweek;
Lori's fake flowers are faded and tattered;
family try keeping them from being scattered.

Four crosses on Interstate I-95—
a month ago, was a family, still alive.
The crosses say they have life everlasting
Or are they just a sign of their passing?

White Crosses mark the spot
Where they made their final earthly stop
It was, for each, a fateful day
when their lives were swept away.

I Saw Heaven Opened

Mount your horses and follow our Lord
As we ride with the King of Glory
with His many crowns and blood-stained robe,
we will see an end to the story.

A broad banner across his chest and thigh
Reads Lord of Lords and King of Kings.
When we get to the valley where the armies wait
An angel stands, shining in the sun, and sings.

We will watch in awe as He swiftly moves
to cast the False Prophet and the Evil Beast
into the burning lake, and slay the unrighteous
And watch the birds come down to feast.

He will stand again on the Mount of Olives
as He promised when on the earth he trod;
and proclaim the world free for a thousand years
For his name is the Word of God.

I MUST

I must
post on Facebook, LinkedIn, Tumblr,
Instagram, Snapchat, Goodreads, Quora,
and oh, I must Tweet today—
how many times—and will it matter?
You see, I have a book and it must be out there
but is this what I must do to get people to pay
    attention?

I must
listen to both sides of a political argument
otherwise I am not being fair (according to them,
    whoever "they" are)
but I hate that no one says what I actually think.
Am I weird? (shut up, you!)
So that is why I do not engage with "them"
I feel like a hermit or an outcast and
I want to hide and not go out anymore
but that would be construed as being reclusive,
which is socially unacceptable (probably).

I must
keep my left-wing friends away from my right-
    wing friends
(especially on social media) so it doesn't get ugly and my
    other friends
don't *unfriend* me because I allowed that stuff
    on my posts.
I really just wanted to keep up with my friends and
    acquaintances
and reconnect with people from 30 years ago, because
    that is fun (right?)
I want to show them that I became something, but that
    is a lie . . .
and let them see how busy I am—make them think I'm
    working—which I'm not.

I must
rethink all of this—I am tired.

POETRY

Poetry is thinking and drinking
and maybe writing while crying.
It is thought out, not bought out—
feels like dying while still trying.

Poetry is personal and terminal—
guts spilled out on a page—
some prophetic; some pathetic
or thoughts filled with rage.

Form is thought to be the norm
by some poetry snob.
But free flowing thoughts
can also do the job.

What you're saying as you're braying
that poetry must rhyme
is that you've no clue what we do
with our sweat, blood and time.

TEA ROSE

"Can we make tea from a tea rose?"
A child's question I could answer not.
"Let's see," said I, and tore some petals
as the water on the stove got hot.

"They smell heavenly when you cut them
so I can't see why they wouldn't make
a nice drink for us to enjoy in winter
or in summer, our thirst to slake."

We enjoyed a few cups after I brewed it
but won't do that again any time soon.
While a cup a day has beneficial effects,
more will keep you in the bathroom.

Prima Donna

Your Petals . . . Oooh
Your Fragrance . . . Ahhh
Your Beauty . . . Ohhh.
But why your thorns?
Are you that insecure?

GROWTH

Behold, a rose;
it steadily grows;
yet we expect more.
What is that for?

Is it not enough
that it shows its stuff
and gives a perfume
noticed on entering a room?

A Lighter Shade of Purple

I watch my bruises
change colors each day.
After two weeks they still
haven't gone away.

The seat belt cut
a large purple path
across my chest; I see
each time I take a bath.

Both knees slammed
hard into the dash.
My ears became numb
from sounds of the crash.

I understand most of the things
from this particular gaffe,
But why did a bruise
show up on my calf?

GEEZER

I had a thought—
it went away.
I had a wake
for it today.

It came, it went;
I could not recall
what I had thought
before at all.

I mourn this thought
as though a friend.
So many thoughts
have found such an end.

PIECE OF PAPER

We're already married in our hearts
and everyone can see our devotion.
Our souls know it to be true
so, what is the magic potion?

Why bother with the piece of paper
and put on the golden rings;
why go through the ceremony
if you already know these things?

A piece of paper, signed and sealed
is more than it appears to be.
It is more to announce to the world
about what you mean to me.

MENAGERIE OF MEMORY

A Tale of Two Horses

My horse has more character than yours,
while, yours gets many more miles.
But, yours pollutes the whole atmosphere
while mine leaves neat, little piles.

Yours is made on a production line;
mine is made one at a time.
I can still ride in pretty high style
without all the grease and the grime.

Yours has good acceleration;
I've got spurs on the back of my boots.
When mine makes a noise, she whinnies;
all yours does is sit there and toots.

To speed up, you step on a pedal,
but, with mine, I just give her the slack.
While it's nice to have all the power,
I'd rather have the love I get back.

THE CHICKEN

I often buy a chicken at the nearest grocery store;
the kind already cut up, which is oft three bucks or more.
This contains a neck and gizzard stuffed away inside;
a heart and liver are also there with the bird besides.

I'm always surprised at what I find more times than I can tell;
Two livers and two hearts are there and a great big neck as well.

The chicken only weighed three pounds—the neck was never hers;
two hearts, two livers, no bird owns; some ire within me stirs.
I wonder why the chicken should cost so much while rearranged?
Are we the victims of a trick, or has the chicken changed?

THE LION
(AN ODE TO OGDEN NASH)

The lion is a kind of cat,
but, not the kind you like to pat.
His mouth is big and opens wide,
and has lots of teeth inside.
Unless I know that he is stone,
I leave the lion quite alone.

THE BEGGAR

Those soft brown eyes looked up at me;
he rubbed his head against my knee
and watched each mouthful that I took,
reproaching me with just a look.
So, I finally dropped a tiny feast,
(acknowledging this lowly beast)
expecting him to mark this day . . .
He sniffed at it and walked away!

RASCAL

Rascal yawns, opens her jaws,
stretches her legs and shows her claws.
Then she begins to wash her face,
stiffens her body with leisurely grace.
Shows her sharp teeth, stretching her lip;
a slice of a tongue turned up at the tip.
Lifting herself up on delicate toes,
she arches her back as high as it goes.
She lets herself down with particular care,
and pads away with her tail in the air!

TED AND ME

I gotta have something to hold onto at night
even though he's just a Teddy Bear.
But he's more than synthetic stuffing
for each night I comb and brush his hair.

I cry alone with him in the darkness
and he hears me with his little pout;
but he always makes me smile at him
because he lets his tongue hang out.

I still tell him bedtime stories
when no one is around.
He listens intently to every word
and never makes a sound.

Spring Momma

If March showers bring April flowers
what do April showers bring?
It brings up bugs like ants and grubs
and momma bird begins to sing
for it means food for her hungry brood
chirping back in their nest.
In a week or so, they'll be ready to go
and momma can get some rest.

Down Under

Sammie's a shy cat
especially with the dog
who smells her and looks
for her down under the bed
and down under the sofa.

KIT—A HAIKU REMEMBRANCE

1. Kit washes her face
   then arches her back high
   slowly and with grace.

2. Watching me eat fish;
   each mouthful that I dare take,
   not getting her wish.

3. Claws in and claws out;
   rolls over, shows her belly;
   pads off in full pout.

TIGER AND HONEY

Tiger was my cat, Honey belonged to my sister.
Honey was sweet, but I was not attached—
I had my own cat to roughhouse with.
But mother thought Tiger was too rough
and I came home one day to find him gone.
I hated Honey—and maybe sis—from that day on;
Tiger was my cat, Honey belonged to my sister.

ODE TO FAKE FUR

Goodbye to Sleepy, a big white bear with closed eyes
that I took to bed at night as a child as a favorite prize.
George was a tan bear with interchangeable bow ties.

Goodbye to Twinkle Toes, a somersaulting monkey.
Arfy, a windup pup, barked, tail wagged, quite spunky.
Chuckles was a hare who dressed in 60s colorful funky.

Goodbye to the big black poodle that I never
    even named,
but put rhinestones 'round his neck because I
    felt ashamed.
But he sat on my pillow until by someone else,
    was claimed.

Goodbye Fluffy, a gray kitten who spun circles twirling
    a little ball
and Everett, a bear matching Senator Dirksen, and sat
    against the wall.
This is an ode to my favorite fake fur friends when I was
    very small.

My Exercise Routine

I have a pup whose name is Bailey
who must be walked five times daily;
round and round and round the block,
round and round and round the clock.

Not a thing will escape her eye
cat, squirrel, lizard, or butterfly.
All make her pull the leash quite hard
til we get back into our yard.

It does not matter the time of day,
she sees these critters and wants to play.
I could change our path to a different route;
but it makes me smile, cuz she's so darn cute.

Stanford, P. (2020) *Variegated Verses in a Millennial Age.*
Florida: Independently published.

THE CLIMBER

Arthur used to climb the fence,
why he did this made no sense.
He had everything a dog might need
air-conditioned house, love, and feed.

When he went into the yard
we watched him struggle very hard
to climb chain link to the other side.
What he could not do was get back inside.

Once out, he'd wander the streets
and when he was done looking for treats
he'd be waiting for us, quite alive
lying down at the end of our drive.

One day he climbed out and did not return
For days we wondered and soon would learn
he'd been hit by a car and crawled under a tree
in a nearby lot, he didn't hear us, and we didn't see.

After several more days of calling his name
out from the brush he finally came
with asphalt pebbles in his head
I cleaned them all out and put him to bed.

LOST

I heard the pitiful mewing
as I parked at my part time job
but did not see what emitted
the sound, so desperate, unceasing.

In front of the store was planted
with shrubs to the walk by the road.
There, a scared, tiny lost kitten,
so gaunt, it must not have been fed
since its birth a few days ago.
Did mother abandon him there?

A box that once held cans of paint.
now held towels in its bottom
for Ace, named for where he was found
he'd now have a chance to get well.

He went home with me that same night.
Food devoured—purring, content.
The wobbly kitten rose in thanks,
but cutely fell back down, eyes closed.
Back at work the following day
all hoped he'd live through his trauma.

I went home and stroked little Ace
and spoke, as he happily purred.
I went to get him a small treat—
he'd died with a smile on his face.

MISNAMED

Snickers was a beautiful cat
named after a favorite candy bar
he had caramel colored stripes and
a sold caramel chest, sweet eyes.

But we should have named him "Shoes"
or "Sneakers," for his foot fetish.
He buried his face in my husband's slippers
and fell soundly asleep.

Love bites to my husband's feet
were frequent as he tried to put on his socks.
When arising, we could not kick the shoes
as he would be curled up among them.

Nemo was as different as he could be.
He was Captain Nemo, not named after a clown fish.
Silver and gray stripes with a solid gray chest.
He often had a crazed look, the imp.

He should have been named "Shadow"
or "Lights" because he chased both.
That began when a friend was over and
his glasses cast lights on the wall.

Nemo attacked the wall in the dining room
as our friend moved his head all around for fun
giggling like a child at the activity.
Later, he took off his glasses to move them around.

Nemo was always more active than Snickers
It was as though Snickers was waiting for Nemo
to report back to him about the value of an activity
I miss you both, Shadow and Shoes.

EVELYN BLYLER'S POETRY

THE BUMBLE BEE
1926 (AGE 10)

One day I saw a bumble bee
and what do you think he said to me?
He said, "I know where the flowers grow
and where the pretty streams all flow.

"If some flowers you want to pick
come with me and come right quick."
Out in the meadow where the flowers are at play
I sip their honey all through the day
from buttercups made of gold
and the daisies, very bold
nodding at each other.

REALIZATION
APRIL 12, 1933

What thou didst hold
in thy strong hand
could be broken or saved
at thy command.

Those treasured hours
so precious to me
are as the flowers
broken by thee.

Moments of silence
neither speaking a word
and my heart singing
songs ne'er to be heard.

Yet these visions seem
to vanish at thy touch
and I realize my dream
has hoped too much!

PRAYER FOR LOVE
DECEMBER 1, 1933

Oh may my love be quiet and still
that my tired mind may take its fill
of holy thoughts—God-given things
and my soul rise up on heavenly wings.

SURETY
JUNE 25, 1934

Changing, ever changing
are my thoughts' strange hue—
it seems I never have a chance
to really think things through.

When finally, I do decide
that such a thing is so,
a newer thought just comes along
and the old one has to go.

Yet deep inside of me, I'm sure—
as sure as I can be
that there remains that something
which is so a part of me!

This spark of soul within me
is my test for all that's true;
it is my rule which measures
every single thing I do.

Though my thoughts are not yet settled,
it is the beacon light
which points the way before me
and guides me through the night.

I cannot hide or cover it
no matter how I try;
for all I am and do declare
that this little thing is I.

LITTLE THINGS
(TO BOB) AUGUST 29, 1934

Heaven is in the little things
that dear ones say and do
which lighten tired hearts and sing
glad songs the whole day through.

A smile may free a heart from bars
it raised against the world
and heal the jagged scar that mars
its beauty yet unfurled.

When love sends thus its glorious ray
think not its work is done
until again it is passed on
to another needy one.

PRAYER FOR PEACE
NOVEMBER 8, 1934

May perfect love abolish fear
and peace abide forever here,
bestowing with its soft caress
its blessing of true happiness.

DREAMS
JULY 5, 1935

Dreams do not vanish with the dawn;
through all life they linger on.
Waking or sleeping, they're a part of me
planning the future that is to be.

They look at the present with eyes serene
seeing naught that is false or mean.
Nothing but beauty and peace and love
sent here on Earth from realms above.

A BLESSING
JULY 28, 1935

God bless you, my beloved—
(What depth of meaning there!)
"God bless you, dear, and keep you,"
is my eternal prayer.

FAITHFUL
DECEMBER 2, 1935

This little dog named Faithful
is all his name implies;
he'll stand upon your desk and watch
with bright and shinning eyes.

The movements all around you
and, if by chance he'll see
that Dick's machine is idle
he'll bark with joyous glee.

Then you may scurry over there
and press with skillful ease
the various combinations
of those little magic keys.

Motionless, he'll stand there
proud and happy, you can see;
for his watchings are rewarded
by your little victory.

Remembrance
February 8, 1936

"Let me help you, mother."
He said those words so dear.
I never shall forget them—
They daily grow more clear.

To a stranger, he addressed them
and offered her his arm.
With his young strength to cling to,
he guided her from harm.

You say it was a little thing—
yes, but the thought was there;
and his small act of kindness
was like unto a prayer.

Oh, God, his heart was tender,
as Thou dost surely know.
His smile was like the sunshine
which maketh all things grow.

Oh, grant that he may ever
keep that vision of the light
which everyone shall guide him
through deepest shades of night.

And for myself, Dear God, I ask
that my heart, too, may be
enkindled with the precious flame
of love for men, and Thee.

The Immortality of Days May 31, 1936

There are days that never perish
as long years pass us by;
for the memories that we cherish
in our treasured house do lie.

Hours of gladness and rejoicing;
hours of poignant pleasure filled
shall stay with us until our hearts
by Death's kind hand are stilled.

Oh, the blessing of those memories—
how they calm and heal the soul!
And our hearts again are lifted
ever nearer to our goal.

To Kermit
April, 1940

Dear friend, I cannot write in rhymes
all that my heart does feel;
for I can't find the proper words
my meanings to reveal.

Thoughts of you bring pleasure
into my heart and mind;
for in abundant measure
companionship, I find.

A precious gift you give to me—
the thoughts that we can share,
which, like a true friend's handclasp,
seems to say, "I'm there."

UNTITLED
SEPTEMBER 21, 1941

Beloved, you are ever
with me night and day—
In all the things I see and hear,
in all the prayers I say.

Your presence is a thing
of mingled joy and pain.
For 'tiz of remembering—
then you are gone again.

REFLECTIONS
OCTOBER 30, 1943

I see my Love in the glory
of the sunset in the sky;
I see my Love in everything,
which lifts my heart on high.

Sweet music which enthralls my ear
and makes my soul rejoice,
is filled with countless memories
and echoes with his voice.

All beauty which enchants me
repeats the same refrain:
"My heart remembers, oh so well—
Dear Love, come back again!"

My Wish
Not dated

This verse, though poor, will let you know
that what I wish for you
is joy—not only for today,
but each day, all life through.

PIETRY—A LITERAL LITERARY FEAST

THE PIEM

Mains & Meats

A Cheap Trip to Mexico
A Culinary Ode
Gluten Free Delight
Gun One, Pig None
Meat Pie Madness
Turkey Day Leftovers

Eat Yur Veggies!

Tears of Joy
Tomato-y Takeover
Veggie Pie Villanelle

Just Desserts

A Hug from Above
American As . . .

THE PIET

Renee Garrison
Gina Edwards
Melody Barton Bragg
Lyla Ellzey
Mark Barie
Judy Ray

Pat Stanford
Pat Stanford
Pat Stanford

Dana Brown
Elizabeth Babski

THE PIE

Taco Pie
Spaghetti Pie
Quiche
Haslett Meat Pie
Tourtiere
Turkey Pot Pie

Onion Pie
Tomato Pie
Vegetable Pie

Sugar Creme
Apple (Gluten Free)

MAINS & MEATS

A CHEAP TRIP TO MEXICO

Renee Garrison

If your budget won't allow
A trip to Mexico,
A short drive to the grocery store
Will yield a unique taco.

Don't hold it in your hands.
(You can use a fork and knife!)
Such a civilized way to add
Some spice to your life.

If spicy foods intrigue you,
Try this Taco Pie.
With its cheese and beans and meat
Es muy bueno—aye, yi, yi!

Taco Pie

Preheat oven to 350⁰.

1-pound ground beef or turkey
1 package Taco seasoning mix
1 small can tomato sauce
1 can refried beans
1 package grated cheddar cheese
1 7-ounce bag Fritos Corn Chips

Brown meat and mix in 1/2 can tomato sauce and taco seasoning. Set aside. Mix refried beans with rest of tomato sauce. Line pie pan with Fritos (like a crust), top with meat mixture, then spread the refried beans. Sprinkle with cheddar cheese and crushed Fritos on top. Bake for 20–25 minutes, until cheese melts and Fritos are crispy.

A Culinary Ode
(Aunt Jan's Spaghetti)

(Can be sung to the tune of "On Top of Spaghetti")

Gina Edwards

My Aunt Jan's spaghetti, all covered with cheese.
It is the world's finest. My family agrees.
The first time I ate it, I was probably nine.
Even back then, though, I knew it was fine.

Then as I got older and I learned to cook,
I wanted Jan's dish in my kitchen cookbook.
So when I got married, Aunt Jan gave to me
all of her best wishes and her recipe.

"The noodles are broken. It's made in a pot."
My new hubs protested, "A pie this is not."
"The sauce is real tasty, all covered in cheese.
But there are no meatballs to lose with a sneeze."

It stayed in my cookbook. I fixed it a lot.
But then it got lost and I somehow forgot.
When dear Pat first called me about her project,
"But I'm not a baker," I had to object.

"I am not a baker. Although I can cook,
nothing that I have would go in your book."
She wanted a poem to go with the pie.
"But I'm not a poet." I thought I would die.

Then I thought of spaghetti all covered in cheese.
I'll put pie in quote marks, so she'll take it. Please.
Though I'm stretching the rules 'bout poems and pies,
if you like spaghetti, just give it a try.

Baked Spaghetti "Pie"

1-1/2 pounds ground round
2 onions, chopped
1 clove garlic, minced
1-1/2 teaspoons salt
1/4 teaspoon pepper
1 to 2 tablespoons Italian seasoning blend
1 teaspoon chili powder
2 8-ounce cans tomato sauce
3 cups water (or chicken broth)
1 cup stewed tomatoes
8 ounces of uncooked spaghetti
1 to 1-1/2 cup cheddar cheese, shredded

Brown meat, onion, and garlic. Stir in seasonings, tomato sauce, water, and stewed tomatoes. Cover and simmer for 25 minutes. Break spaghetti. Alternate layers of spaghetti, sauce, then cheese in a 6-quart casserole, ending with cheese on top. Cover and bake at 350^0 for 30 minutes. Remove the cover and bake 15 minutes longer until cheese is lightly browned.

GLUTEN FREE DELIGHT

Melanie Barton Bragg

Gluten free quiche is quite tasty
Eggs, cheese, and almond milk combine
Although the prep process is not hasty
And the ingredients may not rhyme
Rice flour makes a crumbly crust
Almond flour works the best
Ice water added is a must
for the first bite to pass the test.

Quiche
(Gluten Free)

Makes two 8-inch pies

8 eggs
2 cups of shredded cheese
1 cup of Almond milk
2 cups of broccoli cooked
1 cup of cooked bacon or ham
1/3 cup of chopped onion
Dash of red pepper
1/2 teaspoon of Paprika
Salt and pepper to taste

Whisk together eggs, cheese, and milk. Blend in broccoli and spices. Pour into a gluten-free premade pie crust.

Bake 425^0 for 15 minutes then 350^0 for thirty minutes or until firm.

Let set about 10 minutes before cutting and serving.

GUN ONE, PIG NONE

Lyla Ellzey

Squealing loudly, the pig ran.
The man with the gun took his stand.
Bang went the gun,
down went the pig.
What to make with this one?
It'll be something big.

Innards cooking in a pot.
Gosh, it makes an awful lot!
Liver, lights, and bits of heart
sounds bad but are really good.
With a fork, I will do my part.
Could I eat it? Yes, I would!

Haslet Meat Pie
(Pork Organ Meat Pie)

Order from butcher: 1 fresh or frozen pork heart, 1 fresh or frozen pork liver, 1 fresh or frozen pork lung (the lights), 1 2-pound fresh pork butt roast

1 extra-large yellow onion (or 2 large)
1 tablespoon salt
1/2 tablespoon ground black pepper
4 cups water
2 eggs beaten
2 folded refrigerated pie crusts

Cut heart, liver, and lungs into ¾ in cubes and coarsely chop pork butt. Dice onion.

Measure 2 cups of the lungs, up to 2 cups of the heart, 1 cup of the liver and 2 cups of the pork butt.

Place all ingredients in a heavy pot and bring to boil and continue on high boil for several minutes to blend flavors. Skim off the foam and turn the heat down to simmer and cook for an hour or more until a thick rich stew forms.

Lightly grease 8 x 8 deep dish pie or cobbler pan, unfold and fit one layer of refrigerated pie crust in bottom of pan. With slotted spoon transfer cooked meats to pan. Taste and adjust salt if necessary

When filled, spoon out excess moisture. Lay top pie crust atop stew and crimp the edges with bottom crust. Cut 4 or 5 slits in the top crust for steam. Using a brush (or small clean paint brush), paint the beaten eggs on top crust.

BAKE at 350⁰ for one hour. Lay strips of foil around the edges if browning too quickly. If doughy, bake longer until dryer and golden brown.

MEAT PIE MADNESS

Mark Barie

Once upon a time, I made a meat pie
but soon discovered that talent is a must.
My wife made it often, so I thought I could too
but there is a trick in making the crust.

My crust tasted like old wet cardboard
and required a set of good teeth to chew.
But the minced meat filling wasn't bad—
it just looked like watery beef stew.

The biggest regret was in my offspring:
the little bastards laughed at my masterpiece.
You'd think they'd at least try to be polite
and try one bite for old dad, at the very least.

But they just poked at with their forks
and pretended they were stuffed.
In twenty-five years of food and drink,
I've never known them to have enough.

One look at my meat pie and suddenly
they became epicurean aficionados.
They even offered to do the dishes
as if that would ease my woes.

So, from the business of making pies
I have since retired.
No new children you can accuse
me of since having sired.

But one day when my family least expects it
there'll be another meat pie for them to eat,
and if one of them complains about how it tastes
I will kick them in the ass, with both of my feet.

Tourtiere
(Canadian Meat Pie)

This is a recipe for a 2-crust pie

Preheat the oven to 400°.

1/2 pounds lean ground beef
1/2 pounds lean ground pork
1 medium onion, finely diced
1 medium potato, finely diced
Approximately 2 cups water
1/4 teaspoon clove
1/4 teaspoon cinnamon
1/4 teaspoon poultry seasoning

Sautee the onion in butter.

Combine all ingredients together in a heavy skillet.

Cook over medium heat for 20 minutes, stirring constantly.

Pour the mixture in an unbaked pie shell and add the top pie crust.

Bake at 400° for 35 minutes or until done.

TURKEY DAY LEFTOVERS

Judy Ray

It's Thanksgiving and that means leftovers—
mashed potatoes, sweet potatoes, veggies,
luscious home-made cranberry sauce,
cornbread sausage dressing, silky gravy,
and best of all—turkey!

It's Thanksgiving and that means pies—
savory pies with
lacey, flaky pie crust.
Yum, are you drooling yet?

It's Thanksgiving and that means full bellies—
heavy eyelids while football games play,
while little ones run in and out.
Families eating turkey now,
still eating turkey for weeks later.

Turkey Pot Pie

Using your Thanksgiving leftovers, cut up turkey and pre-boiled potatoes into small bite size pieces. Put leftover gravy in a pan. *(Make more if you don't have enough.)* In a pot, add whatever leftover vegetables you have, and heat with a little ground sage, salt, and pepper. Make your crust or use a pre-made deep-dish pie shell. Add the turkey and vegetables to the shell and bake at 350° for 30 minutes or until the crust is brown. To make a fresh crust:*(Recipe makes 2 crusts and cannot be halved since it calls for only 1 egg)*

Whisk 2-1/2 cups all-purpose flour, 1 teaspoon salt, and a dash of sugar together in a medium bowl. With a pastry cutter, cut 1/2 cup vegetable shortening and 1/2 cup cold butter into the flour mixture until it resembles coarse meal with pea sized pieces of butter.

Lightly beat one egg, then add it to 1/4 cup water and 1 tablespoon vinegar. Add the water to the dry ingredients and mix just until the dough comes together. Divide in half. Form into 2 disks. Wrap in plastic wrap and refrigerate for at least 30 minutes.

Once chilled, remove one disk at a time and roll out into a 12-inch circle. Do this between two sheets of wax paper so you don't have to flour the work counter. Transfer the dough to a 9-inch pie dish. Trim the edges and crimp. Poke the bottom of the crust with a fork several times.

For a fully baked crust Preheat the oven to 350°. Line the crust with parchment paper. Fill with pie weights or dried beans, about half to 2/3 full. Bake to 20 minutes. Remove from the oven and carefully remove the paper and weights. Return the crust to the oven and bake an additional 10 minutes or until golden brown.

EAT YER VEGGIES!

This course provided entirely by the author
since everyone else apparently only eats meat and dessert.

TEARS OF JOY

Pat Stanford

My dear onions, why do you make me cry?
All I am trying to do is make you into a pie.
Your scent lingers on my fingers as eyes recover.
You blind me with tears, but you are no lover.

As your translucent rings begin mixing with butter,
anticipation builds, making my heart start to flutter.
Eggs and sour cream are added to the creamy mixture
only a shell remains to complete this lovely picture.

I anxiously await while you bake to a pie of perfection
while family may think I am making a confection.
But I know what my tears from before will now bring—
tears of joy, contented gut, as my heart begins to sing.

Onion Pie

Preheat oven to 450⁰.

9-inch pie crust
2 1/2 pounds onions, sliced thinly
3 tablespoons butter
3 eggs
1 cup sour cream
Salt & pepper to taste

Melt butter in a pan, add onions & cook over low heat until translucent.

Combine 3 eggs with 1 cup sour cream and salt & pepper to taste. Heat slowly in a separate pan until blended. Stir mixture into onions. Fill pie shell with the mixture.

Bake at 450⁰ for 10 minutes. Reduce heat to 300⁰ and bake until crust is a light brown (about 1/2 hour).

TOMATO-Y TAKEOVER

Pat Stanford

I wanted a pizza late one night
but had no dough, which is a must.
In the back of the freezer—there it was
a leftover two-pack of pie crust.

Now to find something tomato-y
that would make this whole thing work,
I found a large can of peeled tomatoes
in the back of the pantry where it did lurk.

I wondered who bought *that* and why?
I pondered, thinking I might yet succeed
and looked online for something to make
I discovered I had all I would need.

Onion, lots of cheese, and mayonnaise
were the only other things I had to include.
Move over pizza . . . a new late-night snack
has become my new favorite comfort food.

Tomato Pie

Preheat oven to 350⁰.

2 small cans (or 1 large can) of whole peeled tomatoes
1/4 cup dried basil leaves (or 10 fresh chopped leaves—for purists)
1/2 cup chopped onion
1 (9-inch) prebaked deep dish pie shell
1 cup grated mozzarella
1 cup grated cheddar
1 cup mayonnaise

Salt and pepper to taste (I found it really didn't need extra salt.)

Slice the peeled tomatoes and place them in a single layer in a colander set in the sink.

Sprinkle lightly with salt and allow to drain for 10 minutes.

Layer the tomato slices, basil, and onion in pie shell. Season with salt and pepper. (Again, you may want to try this without the extra salt.) Combine the grated cheeses and mayonnaise together. Spread mixture on top of the tomatoes and bake for 30 minutes or until lightly browned.

To serve, cut into slices and serve warm. Add sour cream to make it even better!

VEGGIE PIE VILLANELLE

Pat Stanford

Oh, so wanting to choose a healthy meal,
I went looking for a new recipe
that would feed me with comfort and appeal.

With an all veggie pie, I now can feel
that people can't give me the third degree.
Oh, so wanting to choose a healthy meal,

I'll chop, dice, slice, grate, sauté, shred, and peel
and bake for a hearty new jubilee
that would feed me with comfort and appeal.

Waiting for this prize to cool and congeal
I look forward to its taste with much glee.
Oh, so wanting to choose a healthy meal,

Is it wrong to have this wonderful zeal?
I'm looking for new options just for me
that would feed me with comfort and appeal.

This pie is so good, I feel I could squeal;
if you ate it you would have to agree.
Oh, so wanting to choose a healthy meal,
that would feed me with comfort and appeal.

Veggie Pie

This is essentially the tomato pie with a few additives. *wink*

Preheat oven to 350°.

1 9-inch deep dish pie shell, *prebaked*

Microwave for about 4 minutes, each 2 cups chopped broccoli and/or cauliflower (10 ounces frozen packages).

Place 3 Roma tomatoes, peeled and sliced (or use canned, peeled tomatoes and slice them) in a colander in the sink in 1 layer, sprinkle with salt and allow to drain for 10 minutes. Use a paper towel to pat-dry the tomatoes and make sure most of the excess juice is out, so you don't have a soggy crust.

In a large skillet over medium-high heat add 1 tablespoon olive oil 1 small yellow squash, sliced into rings with salt and pepper. Sauté the squash in a single layer for 2–3 minutes on each side or until golden brown. Remove to a paper towel. Add 2nd tablespoon olive oil and repeat with 1 small zucchini, sliced into rings.

Combine 1 cup shredded mozzarella cheese, 1 cup freshly shredded cheddar cheese and 3/4 cup mayonnaise in a bowl.

Place your broccoli, cauliflower, zucchini, squash, and 1/2 cup sliced sweet OR red onion in cereal bowls for ease of assembly.

Layer tomato slices, broccoli, cauliflower, zucchini, squash, and onion on the bottom of the pie shell. Sprinkle 1/4 cup dried basil leaves (or 10 fresh chopped leaves) on top.

Smooth cheese mixture over the top and sprinkle 2 tablespoons parmesan cheese on top of that.

Bake for about 30 minutes or until lightly browned. Allow to cool for at least 10 minutes.

JUST DESSERTS

Where most of you will hang out

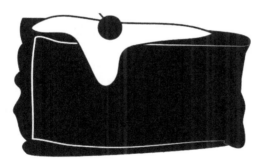

A Hug from Above

Dana Brown

What do you equate with love?
For me it's always been food.
The way it brings people together,
and connects them from the heart.

I never met the woman,
whose recipe this is.
But every time I make it,
I see her in my mind.

It's thick, and rich, and creamy,
Baked in a flaky crust.
It's love inside a pie plate,
And it brings a Grandmother's hug.

Grandmother Reichart's Old Fashioned Sugar Creme Pie

1/2 cup white sugar
1/4 cup brown sugar
2 tablespoons flour
2 cups cream

Mix sugar and flour together, add cream and cook on low heat until it thickens.

CHILL THOROIGHLY

Pour chilled mixture in an unbaked pie shell.

Dot with real butter and sprinkle with nutmeg.

Bake for 20 mins at 400^0.

AMERICAN AS...

Elizabeth Babski

I remember apple pies in
crimped foil pans, perched
on gingham-dressed folding tables—
couldn't fool the church bake-sale ladies.

We ate apple pies from cardboard pouches
deep-fried and lava-filled, they
tasted a little like French fries, but
soda washed them down.

In grandma's tin recipe box
I found evidence of extinct pies
preserved on yellowed index cards
written in a younger hand I never held.

Years ago, you told me apples won't grow
in a Florida yard, though I still tried
before life severed wheat from chaff
and all my saplings died.

Would it make me less patriotic
to buy them bagged in plastic—
waxed, gassed, and shipped cross-country
to bake on the fourth of July?

Gluten-Free Apple Pie

Preheat oven to 375⁰.

You will need:

Pre-made gluten-free pastry crusts, enough for a two-crust pie
3 pounds apples of your choice; peeled, cored, and sliced (enough to mound up high in your pie plate)
3 tablespoons gluten-free flour, more or less
1/2 cup sugar (or to taste)
1 teaspoon cinnamon
1/2 teaspoon allspice
1/2 teaspoon ginger
Juice of 1/2 lemon
1 teaspoon grated lemon zest (opt.)
1/4 teaspoon salt
2–3 tablespoon butter or vegan butter, cut into pieces
Optional: water, egg white, or milk to brush top crust. Also, don't forget the vanilla ice-cream!

Roll out bottom pie crust into a 9-inch pie pan, set aside. In a large bowl, combine apples, sugar, flour, spices, lemon juice, zest, and salt; toss to combine. If it looks too loose, add a bit more flour. Pour into lined pie plate. Apples should mound up high in center (they will cook down.) Dot fruit with pats of butter. Roll out second pie crust and lay over fruit. Cut vents into top crust. Seal crusts together, crimping with thumb and forefinger. Brush top of crust lightly with water, egg white, or milk. Sprinkle with sugar. Place on a baking sheet; this will catch any juices which might bubble over. Bake for 45–60 minutes. Add foil around edges if pastry gets too brown before time is up. Cool for 1 hour before serving.

BIRTHDAY PIE

Rocky Porch Moore

"Why can't you make a pumpkin pie?"
Asked with all the confidence of a little girl grown
accustomed to having her way.
Her curls bounce in time to the tremble
of her pout; hands on hips and broad of stance,
eyes welling with tears that could be spilt
or harden to ice, as she wished.

"Birthdays are cake days," I protested.
"Who ever heard of pumpkin pie on the 4th of July?"

Setting her chin and crinkling her nose;
logic tempering defiance
like the sulfur undercutting the spent sparkler
in her chubby fist.
She thrusts her scepter,
stamping her despot's foot
as she makes her declaration:
"Your birthday can be a cake day, but my birthday is a
Pie Day–Pumpkin Pie!"

And so, we eat midsummer pumpkin pie.

Birthday Pumpkin Pie

1 cup sugar
1/2 teaspoon salt
1 teaspoon ground cinnamon
1 teaspoon ground ginger
1/4 teaspoon ground cloves
2 large eggs, beaten
1 can Libby's pumpkin
1 can evaporated milk
Splash of bourbon (optional)
1 unbaked deep-dish pie shell

MIX all but the pie shell in a stand mixer, adding evaporated milk gradually. Once milk is incorporated, mix in bourbon.

POUR mixture into pie shell and bake at 425^0 for 15 minutes. Lower temperature to 350^0 and bake for 45 minutes or until the pie passes the knife test.

Serve warm with vanilla ice cream.

CHECKMATE!

Ginger Marks

A bit of sugar,
A dab of flour,
A dash of flavor,
and a simple crust,
without the buttermilk,
this pie's a bust.

Buttermilk Chess is the title,
there's no sense to the name,
but, it's not a dessert,
that'll inspire a game.
Put it together,
and a favorite it'll be,
for you, and your entire family.

Buttermilk Chess Pie

2 cup sugar
2 tablespoon all-purpose flour
5 large eggs, lightly beaten
2/3 cup buttermilk
1/2 cup butter or margarine, melted
1 teaspoon vanilla extract
1 unbaked 9-inch pastry shell

Combine sugar and flour in a large bowl; add eggs and buttermilk, stirring until blended. Stir in butter very slowly, add vanilla, and pour into unbaked pastry shell. Bake at 350° for 45 minutes or until set.

Cool in a wire rack. Yield: one 9-inch pie.

CITRUS SUMMER COMFORT

Susan Magers

Looking at Summer skies
and watching temperatures rise.
I need something refreshing, before I die.
Let's make a blueberry lemon pie.

Citrusy freshness fills the air,
Juice and zest are everywhere.
Heavy cream whipped to stiff peaks,
Now add sweetened, soft cream cheese.

Graham cracker crust, right off the shelf.
Five minutes in the oven, as though made by an elf.

Wash the blueberries and pick the stems,
Woody bits that never seem to end.
Mix sugar, water, and berries too,
Reduced to syrupy, sweet blueberry goo.

Layer the lemon and make it smooth,
and the sugary blend for your sweet tooth.
Chill for two hours and you're ready to go,
An easy pie that could win the show.

Blueberry Lemon Creme Pie

Preheat the oven to 375^0.

9-inch graham cracker crust
Cooking spray
3 cups blueberries
3/4 cup cold water
3/4 cup sugar
3 tablespoons cornstarch
1 teaspoon lemon juice
1 cup heavy cream
8 ounces cream cheese, softened
1/3 cup sugar
1 tablespoon lemon zest
2 teaspoons lemon juice

Crust: Place the graham cracker crust on a baking sheet, spray the crust with cooking spray, and heat for 5 minutes. This will make the crust a little crunchy, so it holds up better to the filling.

Blueberry Topping: Wash the blueberries and remove all stems. In a medium-sized saucepan—combine blueberries, water, sugar, cornstarch, and lemon juice. Cook over medium heat, bring to a boil stirring constantly until thickened. (5–7 minutes) Cool completely in an ice bath.

Lemon Creme Filling: Chill a metal mixing bowl and whisk in the freezer for at least 15 minutes.

Beat the heavy cream until stiff peaks form. Add softened cream cheese and sugar, beat until smooth. Mix in the lemon zest and lemon juice until combined.

Assembly: Pour lemon cream filling into the cooled pie crust and spread evenly. Spoon blueberry topping over lemon layer. Garnish with lemon curls, if desired. Chill for 2 hours before serving.

DADDY'S COMFORT CUSTARD

Saundra Kelley

Growing up in depressed times,
my dad loved custard,
trading his baked sweet potatoes
at school for slices of pie.

Later in life
he learned to bake them
to yellow perfection.

Now,
in these troubled times,
I am using his simple recipe
to make one for me.

Once cooled and sliced,
every morsel of simple goodness
a promise of comfort.

Daddy's Custard Pie

Preheat oven to 350^0.

1. Beat three eggs slightly,

2. add 1/2 teaspoon each of nutmeg and salt,

3. 1/2 cup of sugar,

4. 2-2/3 cups of milk

5. Lest we forget, 1 teaspoon of vanilla

6. Beat well, then pour into a baked pie shell, or not.

7. Bake for 35–40 minutes 'til done

When your pie is done, pull it out of the oven, sprinkle nutmeg on top, then put it on a wire rack to cool.

Enjoy!

Friend with a Brown Paper Bag

Kathryn Knight

Her father's work took her family on a journey of the longest kind
to a low country place, untouched by progress, still lagging behind.
The system he built took them from Florida's sunny beaches around
to the deep, flatttened muddy bayous in a Louisiana border town.

She heard her parents say from behind the locked door,
"It's won't be easy for our little blonde girl, anymore."
The statement made her wonder, but she did not mind.
The move was scary and exciting, all at the same time.

For years, it was only family that she had ever known,
sheltered and surrounded by generations of her own.
She was looking for a new friend or maybe even more.
So, she left her mother's refuge and went out to explore.

Her mother said. "Take care; you're not from these parts."
The words did not attach and went forth with a racing heart.
A drastic change to eyes and ears, and voices of a different kind.
She continued like an innocent, wondering what she might find.

Kindness appeared with a brown paper bag in the hand of a girl,
who was blue-eyed and dark-haired, and gave her skirt a twirl.
She looked back where her mother watched through the window,
but turned back to ask, "What's in the bag? I'd like to know."

Then her new friend said, "Oh, it's for you; it isn't much."
She opened the bag, to find a pecan pie, still warm to the touch.
After a few moments the girls hit it off—new friends were made.
They sat down to chat for hours under a tree's welcoming shade.

When she looked at her new friend's face, it said, "Welcome home,"
and the brown paper bag a sign of welcome wherever you may roam.
Now miles can't separate life-long friends, that took time to grow,
that started with smiles and a warm pecan pie—a recipe both know.

Brown Paper Pecan Pie
via Tracy Vige' of Houma, Louisiana

3 eggs
2/3 cup sugar
1/2 teaspoon salt
1/3 cup butter or oleo, melted
1 cup dark or light Karo syrup
1 cup pecan halves or pieces

Beat eggs, sugar, salt, butter, and syrup, with a rotary beater. Stir in nuts. Pour into pastry shell. Place pie in a large brown paper bag and seal the end of the bag with pins or staple shut. Bake 40 to 50 minutes or until filling is firm.

How To Make a Great Pie

Jane R. Wood

I wanted to make a great pie—
something I always wanted to try.
It would need a good crust,
be flaky, it must,
for which my family would want to die.

I watched the cooks on TV,
the experts in culinary.
I could do this I know
like I saw on their show,
it looked so easy to me.

It didn't turn out so well—
there are stories I could tell.
The apples were sour,
I ran out of flour
and my kitchen now looks like hell.

Baking pies is not in my fate.
Now cooking is something I hate!
But my family thinks I
can make a good pie—
thanks to Publix, they think I'm great!

Mother's Lemon Meringue Pie

One baked pie shell
3 egg yolks
1-1/4 cups of water
3/4 cup sugar
Dash of salt
3 tablespoons cornstarch
1/3 cup fresh lemon juice
1 tablespoon Butter
3 egg whites
Dash of cream of tartar
6 tablespoons sugar

Pie filling: Whisk the 3 egg yolks and set aside. Mix sugar, cornstarch, and salt together in a medium size saucepan. Add water and stir together. Bring to a boil on medium heat, stirring constantly. Simmer until it thickens. Remove from the heat and add a tablespoon of the mixture into the beaten egg yolks to temper yolks so they don't cook. Return the cornstarch mixture to the heat and add the tempered egg yolks, stirring constantly. Add the lemon juice. Then add the butter. Put the lemon mixture in the pie shell and let it cool.

Meringue: Beat the egg whites, gradually adding the sugar and cream of tartar. When the meringue makes stiff peaks, add it to the top of the pie filling, making sure the meringue attaches to the edges of the crust. Use the back of a spoon to create peaks on the meringue.

Bake at 350^0 for 15–20 minutes, until the meringue is nicely brown. Cool before serving.

MEMORY PIE

Jenn Smith

The women sit and cluck like chickens.
In the garden the men joke and keep on pickin'.
The porch swing rocks in a summer breeze.
The kids go on snapping beans and shelling peas.

Aunts, and Grans, and mom too,
Crowd the kitchen with chores to do.
Chopping rhubarb and berry washing
After supper, a pie is coming!

The kitchen swelters as the gossip bubbles
A sure place for a young girl to get in trouble.
Snitching pieces of unrolled dough,
Before I'm swatted—off I go!

To the stalls, my friends I rush to see
Then in the loft I sprawl and dream.
There, adventures soon begin for me
of faraway places and all I'll be.

I close my eyes and start to doze
When from a distance, I hear the calls.
I awake to find that time's passed on
and like my youth, the farm is gone.

I'm going back to those lazy days
Silky manes and tender neighs.
To all the love and memory pies,
I lay back down and close my eyes.

Aunt Peg's Strawberry and Rhubarb Pie

Preheat the oven to 425⁰.

Crust: *makes one double crust*

2 cup all-purpose flour, 1-1/2 teaspoon salt, 2/3 cup lard, 1/2 teaspoon vanilla extract (optional, but nice for a sweet pie vs. savory quiche), 12 (or slightly less) tablespoons ICE COLD water.

Combine flour and salt and mix well. Add 1/3 cup lard and using a pastry cutter or two knives, mix until pea-sized crumbs appear. Add ice water a tablespoon at a time, using a fork to combine the dough. Roll dough into a ball and wrap in plastic wrap. Refrigerate a couple of hours or overnight.

Filling:

4-1/2 cups roughly chopped fresh rhubarb stalks, 3 cups hulled and halved fresh strawberries, 3/4 cup granulated sugar, 1/4 cup cornstarch, 1 pinch kosher salt (about 1/4 teaspoon), 3 tablespoons unsalted butter, egg wash (1 egg beaten with 1 tablespoon water), sugar for garnish (granulated)

Roll dough into a circle just larger than your pie plate. Refrigerate the bottom crust while preparing the filling. Place the chopped rhubarb, halved strawberries, sugar, cornstarch, and salt in a large bowl and toss together to coat the fruit in the dry ingredients. Pour filling into the pie crust. Dot with butter and refrigerate while the top crust is prepared. Roll the second half of the pie dough out to about 3 inches wider than the pie pan. Cut into strips and arrange in a crisscross pattern over the filled pie (lattice style). Trim excess, roll & crimp the edges, brush with egg wash, and sprinkle with sugar.

Bake for 20 minutes at 425⁰, then lower the oven temperature to 350⁰ and bake for an additional 45 to 55 minutes. Cool for 2 hours before cutting and serving.

MUTTERING CHOCOLATE CREME

Dee Christensen, II

Ingredients are the mixture,
the flavor—indeed the fixture
that endeavors
taste with heart.

Oreos, whole milk,
Soften cream cheese
two simple tablespoons of
ample sugar.

And oh, so sweet chocolate
(chopped not thinned)
vanilla with butter, not tinned,
preserved or pasteurized
(Cooks? Keep your eyes
on the that milky smooth final prize!)

When heated,
sweet will greet
cream and butter
like a loquaciously mild stutter

And oh, in the end?
The blend will mutter,
"God, this is so good."

10-Minute German Sweet Chocolate Creme Pie

1 package (4 ounces) Baker's sweet chocolate (German)
1/3 cup Milk
2 tablespoon Sugar
1 pkg (3 ounces) cream cheese, softened
3 1/2 cup Cool Whip, thawed
8-inch graham cracker crust
6–8 Oreo cookies

Heat chocolate and 2 tablespoons of the milk in a saucepan over low heat, stirring until chocolate is melted. Beat sugar into the cream cheese; add remaining milk and chocolate mixture and beat until smooth.

Fold in whipped topping, blending until smooth. Spoon into pie crust. Freeze until firm (about 4 hours) Garnish with crumbled Oreos. Store in the freezer.

ODE TO DEPRESSION'S PIE

Ken Johnson

Loss, that fiendish thief o' life—
Investments transmuted to expenses
As the orchard's fermented yield turns to sour
The seed o' man imperiled to become worm food
Just as the cock's seed and orchid's pod destined for baker's fare.

Hardship, oh road most forlorn—
Daily toil exchanged for meager shelter
Just as the calves' drink churned for oil
Bones cracked, muscles bruised, and sinew strained
As Ceylon's bark milled to dust.

Adversity, life's introduction to your true self—
Ore turned into steel
As śarkarā refined from the field's cane
Willful defiance brings to bloom new fruit
Just as the oven yields pastry.

Ah, vinegar pie!

Vinegar Pie

Preheat oven to 425⁰.

4 farm fresh eggs
3 tablespoon apple cider vinegar
1-1/2 cup cane sugar
1 stick melted butter
1/2 teaspoon Mexican cinnamon (or Allspice)
1 teaspoon Madagascar vanilla extract
1 pinch sea salt
9-inch premade premium quality pie crust in a pie pan

Using an electric mixer, mix first seven ingredients together in a large bowl for five minutes. Pour filling into pie shell and bake for 25 minutes. Serve chilled.

Pookeypsie's Gal

Kay Whitehouse

There once was a gal named Pookeypsie.
with a tendency to get a little tipsy.
Her friends thought she was ditzy
but it was the pies from her kitchey
that she laced with her Fireball Whisky!

Fireball Whisky Cinnamon Roll Apple Pie

Preheat oven to 350°.

Crust: 2 packages refrigerated cinnamon rolls, 8 count

Filling:

8 Granny Smith apples, peeled and cut into small pieces
6 tablespoons butter
1/2 cup white shugah
1/2 cup brown shugah
1/2 cup applesauce
1/4 teaspoon salt
6 ounces Fireball Whisky
2 tablespoon flour (I like self-rising)
1 can creme soda

Topping:

2 tablespoons white shugah; 1 tablespoon cinnamon;1 can refrigerated cinnamon rolls; 2 tablespoons butter

In an 8-ounce glass, place 5 cubes of ice, 1.5 ounces of Fireball Whiskey and creme soda to fill. Stir. Sip.

In a large pot, add diced apples, shugahs, butter, applesauce, nutmeg, cinnamon and salt. Stir in the flour and thicken. Pour in 3 ounces Fireball Whisky; stir and cook a minute longer. Transfer the filling to a bowl to cool.

Pop open those cinnamon rolls and press them into a pie plate. Pour filling into cinnamon roll pie crust. Pack it down good and tight for a nice plump pie! Drop pinches of cinnamon roll dough on top of apple whiskey filling as desired. Bake 20–25 minutes. Carefully remove from oven, sprinkle with cinnamon and shugah topping. Dot with 2 tablespoons. butter. Relax and finish any leftover Fireball and cream soda.

Rainy Day Pies

Zelle Andrews

Laughing with my daughter, fresh key limes, and a rainy afternoon.
A few bowls, a blender, and my vintage measuring spoons.
These are the things you need for a key lime pie.

Crumble your favorite cookies to start the crust.
Mixing it with melted butter is a must.
Use your fingers and press this mixture in Grammie's pie pan.
Tell a few corny jokes, laugh at them, and do it again.
These are the things you need for a key lime pie.

Ten minutes in the oven is all it needs to be toasty.
The best part is next, and it'll be so tasty.
If you have a key lime tree, you better get to pickin'.
You'll need at least a dozen to squeeze and for the samplin'.
These are the things you need for a key lime pie.

Blend sweetened condensed milk, eggs yolks, and key lime juice.
Share funny stories until you cry and need some tissues.
Take a large wooden spoon and sample the batter.
You two will be the only ones eating it, so it doesn't matter.
These are the things you need for a key lime pie.

Pour this delicious mixture in your crust and cook for a few.
Refrigerate promptly afterward so you don't have issue.
The remaining batter will be eaten by your daughter.
Don't even try to sneak a taste or you'll be in deep water.
These are the things you need for a key lime pie.

While your daughter is preoccupied with the sweet batter,
Wash a few dishes, and clean up what splattered
Mix heavy whipping cream, vanilla, and confectionary sugar.
Just these three ingredients, it couldn't be easier.
Top the key lime pie with this sweet goodness.
Refrigerate for twelve hours for maximum deliciousness.

This is how you make a key lime pie.

Key Lime Pie

Preheat oven to 350⁰.

Crust:

Gingerbread, graham crackers, or gingersnaps
2 tablespoons butter

Crush cookies, add melted butter, and mix. *If you like a sweeter crust, you can add a few pinches of sugar.* Press into a pie pan and bake for five minutes or until golden and set. Remove from the oven and set on a cooling rack to cool a bit.

Pie Filling:

1/2 cup lime Juice
2 whole egg yolks (separate and use only the yolks)
1 can (14 ounces) Sweetened Condensed Milk

Mix lime juice, and egg yolks, yes you must separate the eggs, in a mixing bowl. Slowly add the sweet condensed milk and continue to mix on high until the filling is smooth and thick. Pour the filling into your cooled crust and bake for fifteen minutes so that it looks set. Remove from oven and allow it to cool an hour. Then you'll want to cover it with the whipped cream and refrigerate it overnight.

Homemade Whipping Cream:

1 cup chilled heavy cream
1 tablespoon confectionary sugar
1 teaspoon vanilla extract

Make sure the heavy cream as well as your mixing bowl, beater, and any spoon you use are chilled at least fifteen minutes. Combine all the ingredients and blend at a low speed. Slowly increase to high speed. Whip until the mixture has tight swirl marks. Layer it thick over the pie and chill overnight.

About the Author

Pat Stanford 's first volume of poetry, titled *Proverbs of My Seasons: Poetry of Transition* won gold medals in both categories of Poetry and Cover Design in the 2019 Florida Authors and Publishers Association Annual Presidents Book Awards. Back with a second volume of poems, she includes poems that encompass five separate sections, all very different, yet all very fun.

Born in Philadelphia, Pat's farming family moved to Delray Beach, Florida looking for year-round growing seasons when she was a one-year old child. She lived there until a brief stint in the Air Force took her to California.

She graduated Florida State University with a B.S.in Secondary Education, which was never used for its intended purpose. Her creative non-fiction, *Fixing Boo Boo: A Story of Traumatic Brain Injury*, is an account of what happens when a brain-injured sibling comes to live with a sister who doesn't know what that means. It won the gold medal for Florida Non-Fiction in the 2017.

Pat lives in Tallahassee, Florida with her husband, a rambunctious puppy, and a quirky cat. She is working on a second non-fiction.

About the Author

Thank you!

The author trusts you enjoyed this small peek into her world. She would love to hear from you. If you enjoyed reading this, her first book of poetry, please consider leaving a review and share the love of rhythmic expression. For those of you who are not comfortable using your given name, you can use "Avid Reader" instead.

It's simple to leave a review. Go to your favorite online book store listed below and type in *"Motley Miscellaney"* in the search bar.

Click on book icon, then "customer reviews" or scroll to "write a review".

Amazon: https://www.amazon.com

Barnes & Noble: https://www.barnesandnoble.com/

Goodreads: https://www.goodreads.com/author/show/16549074. Pat_Stanford

Do you want even more?

Visit Pat's website to view her other work, purchase additional copies, and see news and upcoming events.

https://www.patstanford.com/

To book Pat to speak at your organization's meetings, conferences, workshops, or book club email her at PublishedPoetPat@gmail.com.

pat.stanford.14   @wordhacker_pat   pat-stanford-33786393   stanford.pat

Additional Works by Pat Stanford

Fixing Boo Boo
A Story of Traumatic Brain Injury

Retail: $17.49 | $6.99
ISBN-13: 978-1-950075-08-9 *(print)*
ASIN: B07VX95SQX

All Barb wanted was to be treated like everyone else. All the family wanted was for her to be safe, especially after a life-changing accident that left her brain-injured. When her husband died, she needed assistance to cope with daily meals and chores. Her sister and brother-in-law encouraged her to sell her house and live with them. They had no idea what dealing with brain injury meant. They found out!

Available online and at your local bookstore. Ask for it today!

Proverbs of My Seasons
Poetry of Transition

Retail: $17.49 | $6.99
ISBN-13: 978-1-9378-0198-4 *(print)*
ASIN: B07NCH11HV

The road travelled is not necessarily a straight and easy one, but weaves through the seasons of life. This poetry collection is reflections shared with the reader—a connection to be made?

Some are raw emotions, some are written tongue-in-cheek, others are about the turbulence of youth written with a youthful perspective, and still others show a more mature person. While one poem may make an immediate connection, another may need to be read again. The author meditates on love, friendship, nature, religion, and some seriously fun things.

I hope you will enjoy the journey.